That's *Doctor* Sinatra, You Little Bimbo!

Doonesbury books by G. B. Trudeau

Still a Few Bugs in the System
The President Is a Lot Smarter Than You Think
But This War Had Such Promise
Call Me When You Find America
Guilty, Guilty, Guilty!
"What Do We Have for the Witnesses, Johnnie?"
Dare To Be Great, Ms. Caucus
Wouldn't a Gremlin Have Been More Sensible?
"Speaking of Inalienable Rights, Amy . . ."
You're Never Too Old for Nuts and Berries
An Especially Tricky People
As the Kid Goes for Broke
Stalking the Perfect Tan
"Any Grooming Hints for Your Fans, Rollie?"
But the Pension Fund Was Just Sitting There
We're Not Out of the Woods Yet
A Tad Overweight, but Violet Eyes to Die For
And That's My Final Offer!
He's Never Heard of You, Either
In Search of Reagan's Brain
Ask for May, Settle for June
Unfortunately, She Was Also Wired for Sound
The Wreck of the "Rusty Nail"
You Give Great Meeting, Sid
Doonesbury: A Musical Comedy
Check Your Egos at the Door

In Large Format
The Doonesbury Chronicles
Doonesbury's Greatest Hits
The People's Doonesbury
Doonesbury Dossier: The Reagan Years

a Doonesbury book by

G B Trudeau.

That's *Doctor* Sinatra, You Little Bimbo!

An Owl Book / Henry Holt and Company / New York

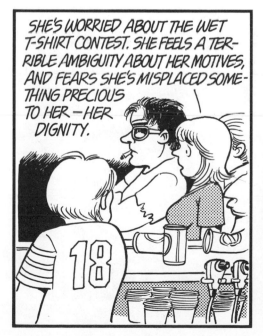

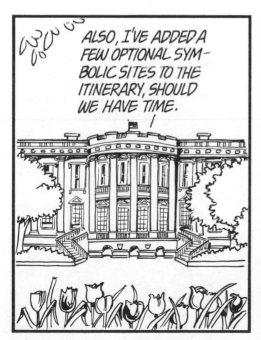

MOMENTS BEFORE AIR FORCE ONE LEFT, WHITE HOUSE IMAGE-MAKER MIKE DEAVER RELEASED THE NINTH AND FINAL VERSION OF MR. REAGAN'S SCHEDULE IN GERMANY.

SAID DEAVER IN A PREPARED STATEMENT, "BY HAVING THE PRESIDENT HONOR NAZI STORMTROOPERS AS WELL AS THEIR VICTIMS, WE FEEL WE HAVE PUT TOGETHER A BALANCED PACKAGE OF SYMBOLS."

HIS FINAL ASSIGNMENT BEHIND HIM, DEAVER IS NOW EXPECTED TO TURN HIS ATTENTION TO SOLICITING BUSINESS FOR HIS NEW P.R. FIRM.

HI. THIS IS MIKE "BITBURG" DEAVER..

⟩CLICK!⟨

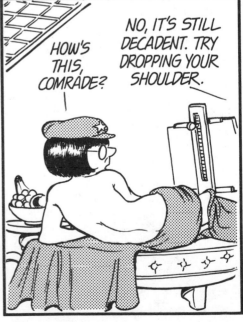

GOOD MORNING, CLASS, AND WELCOME TO THE SHANGHAI ART INSTITUTE'S FIGURE STUDIES PROGRAM.

DUE TO A RECENT RELAXATION OF CULTURAL AUTHORITY, CLASSES SUCH AS THIS ARE ONCE AGAIN POSSIBLE. I URGE YOU TO MAKE THE MOST OF THIS PARTICULAR UPSWING OF THE PENDULUM.

I AM ASSISTED TODAY BY COMRADE HUAN, WHO WILL BE STRIKING THE NEW STATE-APPROVED POSES. IF YOU WILL GO TO YOUR EASELS, WE CAN BEGIN. READY, COMRADE?

READY!

OKAY, CLASS, NOW AVERT YOUR EYES AS MUCH AS POSSIBLE.

©B Trudeau

AS THE MOMENT APPROACHES, TIMMY SEEMS ALMOST OBLIVIOUS TO THE CHARGED DEBATE THAT ATTENDS HIS FATE.

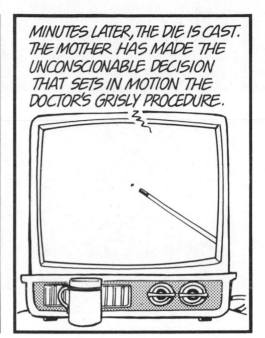

MINUTES LATER, THE DIE IS CAST. THE MOTHER HAS MADE THE UNCONSCIONABLE DECISION THAT SETS IN MOTION THE DOCTOR'S GRISLY PROCEDURE.

THE FINAL SECONDS. BY STUDYING HIS MOUTH THROUGH STOP-ACTION IMAGING, WE CAN DETERMINE TIMMY'S FINAL WORDS, WHICH ARE, ALMOST CERTAINLY, "REPEAL ROE V. WADE."

COMING UP: TIMMY REMEMBERED.

"HIS LOVE OF COUNTRY, HIS GENEROSITY FOR THOSE LESS FORTUNATE, HIS DISTINCTIVE ART..

.. AND HIS WINNING AND COMPASSIONATE PERSONA MAKE HIM ONE OF OUR MOST REMARKABLE AND DISTINGUISHED AMERICANS..

.. AND ONE WHO TRULY DID IT HIS WAY."
– Ronald Reagan
May 23, 1985

©B Trudeau

MEDAL OF FREEDOM RECIPIENT FRANK SINATRA DOING IT HIS WAY WITH TOMMY "FATSO" MARSON, DON CARLO GAMBINO, RICHARD "NERVES" FUSCO, JIMMY "THE WEASEL" FRATIANNO, JOSEPH GAMBINO AND GREG DEPALMA.

"HE HAS CARRIED ON HIS CRAFT WITH DISTINCTION AND HIGH PROFESSIONALISM..

HE HAS APPLIED HIS TALENTS TO THE BENEFIT OF MANKIND..

.. AND TO THE UPLIFTING OF THE HUMAN SPIRIT."
– Citation for honorary degree, Stevens Institute, May 23, 1985

DR. FRANCIS SINATRA UPLIFTING THE SPIRITS OF ALLEGED HUMAN ANIELLO DELLACROCE, LATER CHARGED WITH THE MURDER OF GAMBINO FAMILY MEMBER CHARLEY CALISE.

.. AND ON FRIDAY, I'LL BE IN PALM BEACH. I PROMISED YOUR YOUNG MAN I'D SPEAK TO SOME FRIENDS ABOUT FUNDING THAT NEW SHELTER HE'S SO KEEN ON.

OH, LACEY, RICK WILL BE SO PLEASED! THE SHELTER NEEDS ALL THE SUPPORT IT CAN GET.

WELL, I'M HAPPY TO DO IT, DEAR, BUT I WOULDN'T GET YOUR HOPES TOO HIGH.

IN PALM BEACH, THEY THINK HOMELESSNESS IS CAUSED BY BAD DIVORCE LAWYERS.

GB Trudeau

ON BUDGET? ARE YOU KIDDING, CASSIE? THIS SHOOT IS THE BARGAIN OF THE YEAR!

EVERY SHOT'S BEEN ONE TAKE. IT TURNS OUT ZONKER IS A COMPLETE NATURAL IN FRONT OF THE CAMERA.

WE JUST BLOCKED THE LAST SHOT, AND LET ME TELL YOU, THERE WASN'T A DRY EYE ON THE SET.

GB Trudeau

AND I THOUGHT MR. SUN WAS OUR FRIEND, ZONKER.

HE IS, TOMMY. BUT WE HAVE TO RESPECT HIS POWER!

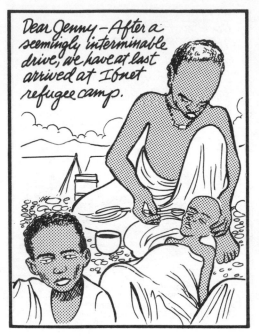

Dear Jenny — After a seemingly interminable drive, we have at last arrived at Ifnet refugee camp.

In trying to come to terms with the suffering here, one has to suspend all previous reference points. No words are adequate to describe this calamity.

The people here have as little comprehension of us as we do of them. Our worlds are totally alien to each other, except, of course, in one notable way..

HE WANTS TO KNOW WHY YOU MOVED FROM REGGAE TO TECHNO-POP.

EXPLAIN TO HIM I NEEDED TO GROW MUSICALLY.

©BTrudeau

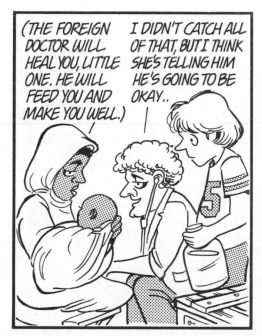

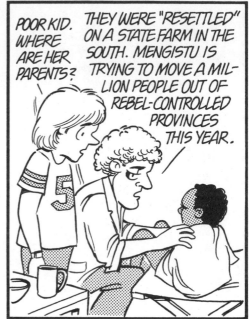

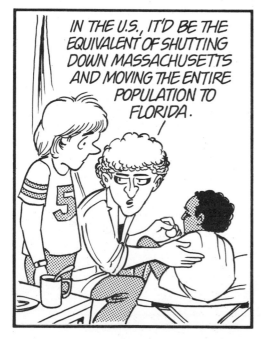

SO WHAT'S THE HOLD-UP, DEAN HONEY?

THE STEWARDESS SAYS THEY WON'T GET OFF THE PLANE, SIR. THEY CLAIM THEY'RE HAPPY WHERE THEY ARE.

DAMN! I KNEW THIS WOULD HAPPEN!

WHENEVER YOU PUT A BUNCH OF HOT-SHOT DRUG DESIGNERS TOGETHER, THE FIRST THING THEY DO IS SWAP COMPOUNDS!

ANYONE HERE WANT TO HELP ME PROMOTE GOOD?

I DO! LET ME GET MY THINGS! IS THIS HOME OR ABROAD?

..AND I'D LIKE TO THANK DR. STAN FILBURN FOR ORGANIZING THE "MOONLIGHT WITH MDMA" THEME PARTY ON THE BEACH LAST NIGHT. WELL DONE, STAN!

OKAY, NOW, TODAY FROM 9:00 TO 9:15, DEAN HONEY WILL BE HOSTING A ROUNDTABLE ON THE ETHICS OF DRUG DESIGNING, AFTER WHICH WE'LL BREAK FOR LUNCH.

AT 2:30, THE MAIN EVENT. THOSE BRILLIANT TWINS FROM USC, DRS. ALBIE AND BUNNY GORP, WILL DEMONSTRATE HOW THEY BEAT THE FEDS WITH THEIR HOT, NEW, TOP 40 HYBRID — "INTENSITY"!

..AND WE JUST REMOVE THIS MOLECULE AND.. VOILA!

LEGAL AS SEA SALT!

POP!

GBTrudeau